TO BE OF USE

*Other books by Marge Piercy*

Poems: HARD LOVING

BREAKING CAMP

4-TELLING (with R. Hershon, E. Jarrett, D. Lourie)

Novels: SMALL CHANGES

DANCE THE EAGLE TO SLEEP

GOING DOWN FAST

# TO BE OF USE

*Marge Piercy*

*Illustrated by Lucia Vernarelli*

DOUBLEDAY & COMPANY, INC., GARDEN CITY, NEW YORK, 1973

ISBN: 0-385-06709-7 Trade
       0-385-06719-4 Paper
Library of Congress Catalog Card Number 73–82240
Copyright © 1969, 1971, 1973 by Marge Piercy
All Rights Reserved
Illustrations Copyright © 1973 by Lucia Vernarelli
Printed in the United States of America
First Edition

Grateful acknowledgment is made by the author to the editors of the following magazines and papers, where many of these poems first appeared, for permission to reprint.

"A work of artifice" first appeared in *Leviathan*, Spring, 1970; "What you waited for" in the Berkeley Tribe, Vol. 6, No. 1, Issue 107, August 14–20, 1971; "The secretary chant" is reprinted by permission of *motive* magazine; "Night letter" first appeared in *aphra*, Vol. 2, No. 2, Spring, 1971 Copyright © 1971 by APHRA, Inc.; "In the men's room(s)" in *aphra*, Vol. 3, No. 3, Summer, 1972 Copyright © 1972 by APHRA, Inc.; "The nuisance" in *The Little Magazine*, Special Woman's issue Vol. 5, Nos. 3 and 4, Fall-Winter, 1971–1972 Copyright © 1971 by *Little Magazine*; "Meetings like hungry beaks" first appeared in *Hellcoal Annual Two*, Hellcoal Press; "A just anger" in *Reflections* Copyright © 1971 by Diana Press; "Back and forth" in CLOWN WAR, No. 2, November, 1972; "High frequency" was originally published in CHELSEA 32; "Apron strings" in *Earth Daughters;* "She leaves" in *Never Mind*, Vol. 1, No. 1; "Unlearning to not speak" was originally published in the KPFA Folio, October, 1971; "The best defense is offensive" in HEARSE, No. 15, 1971; "I will not be your sickness" in HEARSE, No. 10, 1969; "Councils" in HANGING LOOSE, No. 16, Winter, 1971–72; "The winning argument" in HANGING LOOSE, No. 11, 1970; "The woman in the ordinary" is reprinted from BEST FRIENDS ✳2; "Burying blues for Janis" is reprinted by permission of *Up From Under*, Vol. 1, No. 3, January/February, 1971; "Doing it differently" first appeared in ANON 1973; "Icon" in The Transatlantic Review, No. 6, Spring, 1961; "A shadow play for guilt," "The crippling," and "Barbie doll" in *Poems of the People;* "The spring offensive of the snail" in *The Liberated Guardian*, June, 1972; "Right thinking man" is reprinted by permission of EVERYWOMAN, Vol. 3, No. 1,

Issue 29, February, 1972; "The thrifty lover" was published in *Unmuzzled Ox;* "Women's laughter" appeared in ELIMA; "Laying down the tower" first appeared in *off our backs,* an independent women's news journal, March, 1972.

For the give and take
for the feedback between us
for all the times I have tried in saying these poems
to give back some of the energy we create together
from all the women who could never make themselves heard
the women no one would listen to
to all the women who are unlearning to not speak
and growing through listening to each other

# CONTENTS

TO BE OF USE

# I. A JUST ANGER

## A work of artifice

The bonsai tree
in the attractive pot
could have grown eighty feet tall
on the side of a mountain
till split by lightning.
But a gardener
carefully pruned it.
It is nine inches high.
Every day as he
whittles back the branches
the gardener croons,
It is your nature
to be small and cozy,
domestic and weak;
how lucky, little tree,
to have a pot to grow in.
With living creatures
one must begin very early
to dwarf their growth:
the bound feet,
the crippled brain,
the hair in curlers,
the hands you
love to touch.

## *What you waited for*

You called yourself a dishwater blond,
body warm and flat as beer that's been standing.
You always had to stand until your feet were sore
behind the counter
with a smile like an outsized safety pin
holding your lips off your buck teeth.

Most nights alone or alone with men
who wiped themselves in you.
Pass the damp rag over the counter again.
Tourist cabins and roadhouses of the deaf loudmouth,
ponds where old boots swim and drive-in moons.
You came to see yourself as a salesman's bad joke.
What did you ever receive for free
except a fetus you had to pay to yank out.

Troubles cured you salty as a country ham,
smoky to the taste, thick skinned and tender inside
but nobody could take nourishment
for lacking respect.
No husband, no baby, no house, nobody to own you
public as an ashtray you served
waiting for the light that came at last
straight into the windshield on the highway.

Two days later the truckers are pleased.
Your replacement is plain but ten years younger.
Women's lives are shaped like cheap coffins.
How long will she wait for change?

4

## The secretary chant

My hips are a desk.
From my ears hang
chains of paper clips.
Rubber bands form my hair.
My breasts are wells of mimeograph ink.
My feet bear casters.
Buzz. Click.
My head
is a badly organized file.
My head is a switchboard
where crossed lines crackle.
My head is a wastebasket
of worn ideas.
Press my fingers
and in my eyes appear
credit and debit.
Zing. Tinkle.
My naval is a reject button.
From my mouth issue canceled reams.
Swollen, heavy, rectangular
I am about to be delivered
of a baby
xerox machine.
File me under W
because I wonce
was
a woman.

## Night letter

Scalded cat,
claws, arched back and blistered pride:
my friend. You'd have cooked down
my ropy carcass in a kettle for soup.
I was honing my knife.
What is friendship
to the desperate?
Is it bigger than a meal?

Before any mirror or man we jostled.
Fought from angst to Zeno,
sucked the onion of suspicion,
poured lie on the telephone.
Always head on: one raw from divorce court
spitting toads and nail clippings,
the other fresh baked from a new final bed
with strawberry-cream-filled brain.
One cooing, while the other spat.
To the hunted
what is loyalty?
Is it deeper than an empty purse?
Wider than a borrowed bed?

Of my two best friends at school
I continued to love the first Marie better
because she died young
so I could carry her along with me,
a wizened embryo.

But you and I clawed at hardscrabble hill
willing to fight anyone
especially each other
to survive.

Couldn't we have made alliance?
We were each so sure
of the way out,
the way in.
Now they've burnt out your nerves, my lungs.
We are better fed
but no better understood,
scabby and gruff with battle.
Bits of our love are filed in dossiers
of the appropriate organizations.
Bits of our love are moldering
in the Lost and Found offices of bankrupt railroads.
Bits stick like broken glass
in the minds of our well-earned enemies.
Regret is a damp wind
off the used car lot
where most of our peers came to rest.
Now—years too late—my voice quavers,
Can I help?

## *In the men's room(s)*


When I was young I believed in intellectual conversation:
I thought the patterns we wove on stale smoke
floated off to the heaven of ideas.
To be certified worthy of high masculine discourse
like a potato on a grater I would rub on contempt,
suck snubs, wade proudly through the brown stuff on the floor.
They were talking of integrity and existential ennui
while the women ran out for six-packs and had abortions
in the kitchen and fed the children and were auctioned off.

Eventually of course I learned how their eyes perceived me:
when I bore to them cupped in my hands a new poem to nibble,
when I brought my aerial maps of Sartre or Marx,
they said, she is trying to attract our attention,
she is offering up her breasts and thighs.
I walked on eggs, their tremulous equal:
they saw a fish peddler hawking in the street.

Now I get coarse when the abstract nouns start flashing.
I go out to the kitchen to talk cabbages and habits.
I try hard to remember to watch what people do.
Yes, keep your eyes on the hands, let the voice go buzzing.
Economy is the bone, politics is the flesh,
watch who they beat and who they eat,
watch who they relieve themselves on, watch who they own.
The rest is decoration.

### *Absence becomes a fact*

In the warm rain of the shower we splashed and hugged
the soap slipping under our feet.
The water parted on your cock like a mustache.
We had to wade through two inches of water
to the bed where whooping Clean! Clean!
you came into me molten and shimmering.
Every pore sang in a lucid trance.
Trust made my bones luminous
till I ran like a grape with purple juice.
How you were there. You.
That was parting.

A week spent I returned
but have not yet found the way back.
How you charge me for loving you
tax from every charred finger and burnt hair end.
In defeat you do not know how to take strength from me.
Testing, testing, you march on the stage of my breasts
striking poses and hearing their resonance in my belly.

My body is a mirror
where you study out shadings of indifference.
You give me a finger and take it back,
lists of tasks and failures
and your muffled anger showing its head
like a dragon of blood and gold
above the roiled waters.

9

I want us to enter again
the sweat lucid honey and warm coarse bread of intimacy.
I want to be with you.
I want to be with
you.

### *I will not be your sickness*

Opening like a marigold
crop of sun and dry soil
acrid, bright, sturdy.

Spreading its cancer
through the conduits of the body,
a slow damp murder.

Breathing like the sea
glowing with foam and plankton.
Rigid as an iron post
driven between my breasts.

Will you lift your hands
and shape this love
into a thing of good?
Will you permit me to live
when you are not looking?
Will you let me ask questions
with my mouth open?

I will not pretend any more
to be a wind or a mood.
Even with our eyes closed
we are walking
on someone's map.

## The nuisance

I am an inconvenient woman.
I'd be more useful as a pencil sharpener or an adding machine.
I do not love you the way I love Mother Jones or the surf coming in
or my pussycats or a good piece of steak.
I love the sun prickly on the black stubble of your cheek.
I love you wandering floppy making scarecrows of despair.
I love you when you are discussing changes in the class structure
and I'm not supposed to, and it crowds my eyes
and jams my ears and burns in the tips of my fingers.

I am an inconvenient woman.
You might trade me in on a sheepdog or a llama.
You might trade me in for a yak.
They are faithful and demand only straw.
They make good overcoats.
They never call you up on the telephone.

I love you with my arms and my legs
and my brains and my cunt and my unseemly history.
I want to tell you about when I was ten and it thundered.
I want you to kiss the crosshatched remains of my burn.
I want to read you poems about drowning myself
laid like eggs without shells at fifteen under Shelley's wings.
I want you to read my old loverletters.

I want you to want me
as directly and simply and variously
as a cup of hot coffee.
To want to, to have to, to miss what can't have room to happen.
I carry my love for you
around with me like my teeth
and I am starving.

## *The thrifty lover*

At the last moment you decided
to take the bus
rather than the plane,
to squander those hours
staring at your reflection
on a dark window.

Then all night you rummaged
my flesh for some body else.
You pinched and kneaded
testing for ripeness,
suspicious and about to reject me
or knock down the price.

You lectured me like a classroom
on your subjects of the week,
used homilies,
reconditioned anecdotes,
jokes with rebuilt transmissions.
All the time your eyes veered.

What's wrong, I would ask.
Nothing, you would say,
eyes full of nothing.
By the time you left
I went down on my knees
to thank you for not breaking
all my bones.
See, I can hobble away.
That's enough to ask.

## A shadow play for guilt

**1.**

A man can lie to himself.
A man can lie with his tongue
and his brain and his gesture;
a man can lie with his life.
But the body is simple as a turtle
and straight as a dog:
the body cannot lie.

You want to take your good body off like a glove.
You want to stretch it and shrink it
as you change your abstractions.
You stand in flesh with shame.
You smell your fingers and lick your disgust
and are satisfied.
But the beaten dog of the body remembers.
Blood has ghosts too.

**2.**

You speak of the collective.
You speak of open communication
but you form your decisions
and visit them on others
like an ax.
In all of the movement there is nothing to fear
like a man whose rhetoric is good
and whose ambition for himself is fierce:
a man who says *we*, moving us,
and means *I* and *mine*.

3.

Many people have a thing they want to protect.
Sometimes the property is wheat, oil fields, slum housing,
plains on which brown people pick green tomatoes,
stocks in safety deposit boxes, computer patents,
thirty dollars in a shoebox under a mattress.
Maybe it's a woman they own and her soft invisible labor.
Maybe it's images from childhood of how things should be.
The revolutionary says, we can let go.
We both used to say that a great deal.
If what we change does not change us
we are playing with blocks.


4.

Always you were dancing before the altar of guilt.
A frowning man with clenched fists
you leaned cast iron on my breasts to grapple and feed
gritting your teeth for fear
a good word would slip out:
a man who came back again and again
yet made sure that his coming was attended by pain
and marked by a careful coldness,
as if gentleness were an inventory that could run low,
as if loving were an account that would be overdrawn,
as if tenderness saved drew interest.
You are a capitalist of yourself.
You hoard for fantasies and deceptions
and the slow seep of energy from the loins.
You fondle your fears and coddle them
while you urge others on.

Among your fantasies and abstractions
ranged like favorite battered toys,
you stalk with a new item, gutted
from what was alive and curious.
Now it is safe,
private and tight as a bank vault
or a tomb.

## Song of the fucked duck

In using there are always two.
The manipulator dances with a partner who cons herself.
There are lies that glow so brightly we consent
to give a finger and then an arm
to let them burn.
I was dazzled by the crowd where everyone called my name.
Now I stand outside the funhouse exit, down the slide
reading my guidebook of Marx in Esperanto
and if I don't know any more which way means forward
down is where my head is, next to my feet
with a pocketful of words and plastic tokens.
Form follows function, says the organizer
and turns himself into a paper clip,
into a vacuum cleaner,
into a machine gun.
Function follows analysis
but the forebrain
is only an owl in the tree of self.
One third of life we prowl in the grottoes of sleep
where neglected worms ripen into dragons
where the spoiled pencil swells into an oak,
and the cows of our early sins are called home chewing their cuds
and turning the sad faces of our childhood upon us.
Come back and scrub the floor, the stain is still there,
come back with your brush and kneel down,
scrub and scrub again,
it will never be clean.
Buried desires sprout like mushrooms on the chin of the morning.

The will to be totally rational
is the will to be made out of glass and steel:
and to use others as if they were glass and steel.
We can see clearly no farther
than our hands can touch.
The cockroach knows as much as you know about living.
We trust with our hands and our eyes and our bellies.
The cunt accepts.
The teeth and back reject.
What we have to give each other:
dumb and mysterious as water swirling.
Always in the long corridors of the psyche
doors are opening and doors are slamming shut.
We rise each day to give birth or to murder
selves that go through our hands like tiny fish.
You said: I am the organizer, and took and used.
You wrapped your head in theory like yards of gauze
and touched others only as tools that fit to your task
and if one tool broke you seized another.
Arrogance is not a revolutionary virtue.
The manipulator liberates only
the mad bulldozers of the ego to level the ground.
I was a tool that screamed in the hand.
I have been loving you so long and hard and mean
and the taste of you is part of my tongue
and your face is burnt into my eyelids
and I could build you with my fingers out of dust
and now it is over.

Whether we want or not
our roots go down to strange waters,
we are creatures of the seasons and the earth.
You always had a reason and you have them still
rattling like dry leaves on a stunted tree.

## *A just anger*

Anger shines through me.
Anger shines through me.
I am a burning bush.
My rage is a cloud of flame.
My rage is a cloud of flame
in which I walk
seeking justice
like a precipice.
How the streets
of the iron city
flicker, flicker,
and the dirty air
fumes.
Anger storms
between me and things,
transfiguring,
transfiguring.
A good anger acted upon
is beautiful as lightning
and swift with power.
A good anger swallowed,
a good anger swallowed
clots of blood
to slime.

## Right thinking man

The head: egg of all.
He thinks of himself as a head thinking.
He is eating a coddled egg.
He drops a few choice phrases on his wife
who cannot seem to learn after twenty years
the perfection of egg protein
neither runny nor turned to rubber.
He drinks orange juice sweated from migrant labor.
Their children have pot bellies of hunger.
He drinks coffee from the colony of Brazil.
Advancing into his study he dabbles a forefinger
in the fine dust on his desk and calls his wife
who must go twitching to reprimand
the black woman age forty-eight who cleans the apartment.
Outside a Puerto Rican in a uniform
is standing in the street to guard his door
from the riffraff who make riots on television,
in which the university who pays him owns much stock.

Right thinking is virtue, he believes,
and the clarity of the fine violin of his mind
leads him a tense intricate fugue of pleasure.
His children do not think clearly.

They snivel and whine and glower and pant
after false gods who must be blasted with sarcasm
because their barbaric heads
keep growing back in posters on bedroom walls.
His wife does not dare to think.
He married her for her breasts
and soft white belly of surrender arching up.

The greatest pain he has ever known
was getting an impacted wisdom tooth out.
The deepest suffering he ever tasted
was when he failed to get a fellowship
after he had planned his itinerary.
When he curses his dependents
Plato sits on his right hand and Aristotle on his left.
Argument is lean red meat to him.
Moses and Freud and St. Augustine are in his corner.
He is a good man and deserves to judge us all
who go making uncouth noises and bangs in the street.
He is a good man: if you don't believe me,
ask any god.
He says they all think like him.

## The crippling

I used to watch it on the ledge:
a crippled bird.
How did it survive?
Surely it would die soon.
Then I saw a man
at one of the windows
fed it, a few seeds,
a crust from lunch.
Often he forgot
and it went hopping on the ledge
a starving
scurvy sparrow.
Every couple of weeks
he caught it in his hand
and clipped back one wing.
I call it a sparrow.
The plumage was sooty,
sometimes in the sun
scarlet as a tanager.
He never let it fly.
He never took it in.
Perhaps he was starving too.
Perhaps he counted every crumb.
Perhaps he hated
that anything alive
knew how to fly.

## Barbie doll

This girlchild was born as usual
and presented dolls that did pee-pee
and miniature GE stoves and irons
and wee lipsticks the color of cherry candy.
Then in the magic of puberty, a classmate said:
You have a great big nose and fat legs.

She was healthy, tested intelligent,
possessed strong arms and back,
abundant sexual drive and manual dexterity.
She went to and fro apologizing.
Everyone saw a fat nose on thick legs.

She was advised to play coy,
exhorted to come on hearty,
exercise, diet, smile and wheedle.
Her good nature wore out
like a fan belt.
So she cut off her nose and her legs
and offered them up.

In the casket displayed on satin she lay
with the undertaker's cosmetics painted on,
a turned-up putty nose,
dressed in a pink and white nightie.
Doesn't she look pretty? everyone said.
Consummation at last.
To every woman a happy ending.

## *The winning argument*

Once in a while
there were a man and a woman
who lived roundly together.
She made him French toast and muffins
and they rolled and cuddled on the bed.
She insisted that the noises under the floor
came from the sea eating away the foundation
and full of dangerous creatures.
He said they were miles inland,
plagued by mice, and that her imagination
was full of dangerous creatures.

One washed out Moonday he climbed the table
to announce he was tired of French toast,
had purchased an electric muffin machine
and that his favorite Japanese Go master
had declared fucking bad for the health.
He threw her out the door.

She landed in the sea with a splash.
As the sharks ate her toes and nose
she recalled that his Japanese Go master
had died of gout.
As the sharks tore her liver,
she derived satisfaction observing
that the sea was under the house
and that sharks are classified
in all known studies
as dangerous.

## High frequency

They say that trees scream
under the bulldozer's blade.
That when you give it water,
the potted coleus sings.
Vibrations quiver about leaves
our ears are too gross
to comprehend.

Yet I hear on this street
where sprinklers twirl
on exterior carpeting
a high rising whine.
The grass looks well fed.
It must come from inside
where a woman on downs is making
a creative environment
for her child.

The spring earth cracks
over sprouting seeds.
Hear that subliminal roar,
a wind through grass and skirts,
the sound of hair crackling,
the slither of anger
just surfacing.

Pressed against glass and yellowing,
scrawny, arching up to the
insufficient light, plants
that do not belong in houses
sing of what they want:

like a woman who's been told
she can't carry a tune,
like a woman afraid people will laugh
if she raises her voice,
like a woman whose veins surface
compressing a scream,
like a woman whose mouth hardens
to hold locked in her own
harsh and beautiful song.

## Hello up there

Are you You or Me or It?
I go littering you over the furniture
and picking you out of the stew.
Often I've wished you otherwise: sleek,
docile, decorative and inert.
Yet even in daydreams I cannot imagine myself
otherwise thatched: coarse, black and abundant
like weeds burst from the slagheaps of abandoned mines.

In the '50's children used to point and shout Witch.
Later they learned to say Beatnik and later yet, Hippie,
but old grandmamas with Thessaloniki or Kiev in their throats
thought I must be nice because I looked like a peasant.
In college my mother tried to change my life
by bribing me to cut it off and have it "done."
Afterwards the hairdresser chased me waving my hair in a paper bag.
Being done over changed my luck, all right.
The next man who happened was a doctor's son
who quoted the Lord Freud in bed and on the pot,
thought I wrote poems because I lacked a penis
and beat me when he felt ugly.
I grew my hair back just as quick as I could.

Cloud of animal vibrations,
tangle of hides and dark places
you keep off the tidy and the overly clean and the wango upright.
You proclaim the sharp limits of my patience
with trying to look like somebody's wet dream.
Though I can trim you and throw you out with the coffee grounds,
when I am dead and beginning to smell worse than my shoes
presumably you will continue out of my skull
as if there were inside no brains at all
but only a huge bobbin of black wire unwinding.

### The woman in the ordinary

The woman in the ordinary pudgy downcast girl
is crouching with eyes and muscles clenched.
Round and pebble smooth she effaces herself
under ripples of conversation and debate.
The woman in the block of ivory soap
has massive thighs that neigh,
great breasts that blare and strong arms that trumpet.
The woman of the golden fleece
laughs uproariously from the belly
inside the girl who imitates
a Christmas card virgin with glued hands,
who fishes for herself in other's eyes,
who stoops and creeps to make herself smaller.
In her bottled up is a woman peppery as curry,
a yam of a woman of butter and brass,
compounded of acid and sweet like a pineapple,
like a handgrenade set to explode,
like goldenrod ready to bloom.

## *Women's laughter*

1.

When did I first become aware—
hearing myself on the radio?
listening to tapes of women in groups?—
of that diffident laugh that punctuates,
that giggle that apologizes,
that bows fixing parentheses before, after.
That little laugh sticking
in the throat like a chicken bone.

That perfunctory dry laugh
carries no mirth, no joy
but makes a low curtsy, a kowtow
imploring with praying hands:
forgive me, for I do not
take myself seriously.
Do not squash me.

2.

Phyllis, on the deck we sit
telling horror stories
from the *Marvel Comics* of our lives.
We exchange agonies, battles and after each
we laugh madly and embrace.

That raucous female laughter
is drummed from the belly.
It rackets about kitchens,
flapping crows
up from a carcass.
Hot in the mouth as horseradish,
it clears the sinuses
and the brain.

3.
Phyllis, I had a friend
who used to laugh with me
braying defiance, as we roar
with bared teeth.
After the locked ward
where they dimmed her with drugs
and exploded her synapses,
she has now that cough
fluttering in her throat
like a sick pigeon
as she says, but of course
I was sick, you know,
and laughs blood.

# *Apron strings*

So hard for women to believe each other.
Mama said she loved me
then screamed for years
to give me away.
I learned early to lie about boys.

Any breast masks the maternal.
Any dress
can rustle her loose.
Brush of hair, perfume,
wet body smells, blood
touch that first pain.

I am not mothering you,
I am not putting you
inside me for keeps,
I am not going to be afraid
you will swallow me
or break me to mewling child.

I am not doing much yet
that is real
except trying
to see you with me.

## She leaves

Someone you fell in love with
when you were virgin and succulent,
soft and sticky in strong hands.

How you twined over him, rampant
and flowing, a trumpet vine.
How you flourished in the warm weather
and died down to your roots
in the cold, when that regularly came.

Then slowly you began to discover
you might grow on your own spine.
You might dare to make wood.

What a damp persistent guilt comes down
from ceasing to need.
Every day you fight free,
every morning you wake tied
with that gossamer web,
bound to him sleeping with open
vulnerable face and closed eyes
stuck to your side.

You meet others open while awake:
you leap to them. The pain
in his face trips you.
You serve him platters of cold gratitude.
They poison you and he thrives.

What a long soft dying this is between you.
Drown that whining guilt
in laughter and polemics. You were trained
like a dog in obedience school
and you served for years in bed, kitchen, laundry room.
You loved him as his mother always told him
he deserved to be loved.
Now love yourself.

## Unlearning to not speak

Blizzards of paper
in slow motion
sift through her.
In nightmares she suddenly recalls
a class she signed up for
but forgot to attend.
Now it is too late.
Now it is time for finals:
losers will be shot.
Phrases of men who lectured her
drift and rustle in piles:
Why don't you speak up?
Why are you shouting?
You have the wrong answer,
wrong line, wrong face.
They tell her she is womb-man,
babymachine, mirror image, toy,
earth mother and penis-poor,
a dish of synthetic strawberry icecream
rapidly melting.
She grunts to a halt.
She must learn again to speak
starting with *I*
starting with *We*
starting as the infant does
with her own true hunger
and pleasure
and rage.

## Burying blues for Janis

Your voice always whacked me right on the funny bone
of the great-hearted suffering bitch fantasy
that ruled me like a huge copper moon with its phases
until I could, partially, break free.
How could I help but cherish you for my bad dreams?
Your voice would grate right on the marrow-filled bone
that cooks up that rich stew of masochism where we swim.
Woman is born to suffer, mistreated and cheated.
We are trained to that hothouse of exploitation.
Never do we feel so alive, so in character
as when we're walking the floor with the all-night blues.
When some man not being there who's better gone
becomes a lack that swells up to a gaseous balloon
and flattens from us all thinking and sensing and purpose.

Oh, the downtrodden juicy longdrawn female blues:
you throbbed up there with your face slightly swollen
and your barbed hair flying energized and poured it out,
the blast of a furnace of which the whole life is the fuel.
You embodied that good done-in mama who gives and gives
like a fountain of boozy chicken soup to a rat race of men.
You embodied the pain hugged to the breasts like a baby.
You embodied the beautiful blowzy gum of passivity,
woman on her back to the world endlessly hopelessly raggedly
offering a brave front to be fucked.
That willingness to hang on the meathook and call it love,
that need for loving like a screaming hollow in the soul,
that's the drug that hangs us and drags us down
deadly as the icy sleet of skag that froze your blood.

## II. THE SPRING OFFENSIVE OF THE SNAIL

### The best defense is offensive

The turkey vulture,
a shy bird ungainly on the ground
but massively graceful in flight,
responds to attack
uniquely.
Men have contempt for this scavenger
because he eats without killing.
When an enemy attacks,
the turkey vulture vomits:
the shock and disgust of the predator
are usually sufficient
to effect his escape.
He loses only his dinner,
easily replaced.
All day I have been thinking
how to adapt
this method of resistance.
Sometimes only the stark
will to disgust
prevents our being consumed:
there are clearly times
when we must make a stink
to survive.

## Icon

In the chapel where I could praise
that is just being built,
the light bleeding through one window blazons
a profiled centaur whose colors mellow the sun.

See her there: hoofs braced into the loam,
banner tail streaming, burnished thighs,
back with the sheen of china but sturdy as brick,
that back nobody rides on.
Instead of a saddle, the poised arms,
the wide apart breasts, the alert head
are thrust up from the horse's supple torso
like a swimmer who breaks water to look
but doesn't climb out or drown.

She is not monstrous
but whole in her power, galloping:
both the body tacking to the seasons of her needs
and the tiger lily head loft with tenacious gaze.
This torso is not ridden.
This face is no rider.
As a cascade is the quickening of a river,
here thought shoots in a fountain to the head
and then slides
back through those rippling flanks again.

## Some collisions bring luck

I had grown invisible as a city sparrow.
My breasts had turned into watches.
Even my dreams were of function and meeting.

Maybe it was the October sun.
The streets simmered like laboratory beakers.
You took my hand, a pumpkin afternoon
with bright rind carved in a knowing grin.
We ran upstairs.
You touched me and I flew.
Orange and indigo feathers broke through my skin.
I rolled in your coarse rag-doll hair.
I sucked you like a ripe apricot down to the pit.
Sitting crosslegged on the bed we chattered
basting our lives together with ragged stitches.

Of course it all came apart
but my arms glow with the fizz of that cider sun.
My dreams are of mating leopards and bronze waves.
We coalesced in the false chemistry of words
rather than truly touching
yet I burn cool glinting in the sun
and my energy sings like a teakettle all day long.

## Back and forth

My hands keep wanting to open,
to drift like feathers on your back,
to hold your gaze between my palms,
to brood on your nape,
to pull your hips against me.

I don't know how to think it is wrong
that I keep wanting to open
to you, like a door
that goes on swinging in the wind
open and shut
wide and shut
and wide again
with unnecessary bangs.

## We become new

How it feels to be touching
you: an Io moth, orange
and yellow as pollen,
wings through the night
miles to mate,
could crumble in the hand.

Yet our meaning together
is hardy as an onion
and layered.
Goes into the blood like garlic.
Sour as rose hips.
Gritty as whole grain.
Fragrant as thyme honey.

When I am turning slowly
in the woven hammocks of our talk,
when I am chocolate melting into you,
I taste everything new
in your mouth.

You are not my old friend.
How did I used to sit
and look at you? Now
though I seem to be standing still
I am flying flying flying
in the trees of your eyes.

## *Meetings like hungry beaks*

There is only time to say the first word,
there is only time to stammer the second.
Traffic jams the highways of nerve,
lungs fill with the plaster of demolition.
Each hour has sixty red and gold and black hands
welding and plucking and burning.

Your hair crosses my mouth in smoke.
The bridge of arms,
the arch of backs:
our fingers clutch.
The violet sky lights and crackles
and fades out.

I am at a desk adding columns of figures.
I am in a supermarket eying meat.
The scene repeats on the back of my lids
like an advertisement in neon
for another world.

## *To be of use*

The people I love the best
jump into work head first
without dallying in the shallows
and swim off with sure strokes almost out of sight.
They seem to become natives of that element,
the black sleek heads of seals
bouncing like half-submerged balls.

I love people who harness themselves, an ox to a heavy cart,
who pull like water buffalo, with massive patience,
who strain in the mud and the muck to move things forward,
who do what has to be done, again and again.

I want to be with people who submerge
in the task, who go into the fields to harvest
and work in a row and pass the bags along,
who stand in the line and haul in their places,
who are not parlor generals and field deserters
but move in a common rhythm
when the food must come in or the fire be put out.

The work of the world is common as mud.
Botched, it smears the hands, crumbles to dust.
But the thing worth doing well done
has a shape that satisfies, clean and evident.
Greek amphoras for wine or oil,
Hopi vases that held corn, are put in museums
but you know they were made to be used.
The pitcher cries for water to carry
and a person for work that is real.

## *Bridging*

Being together is knowing
even if what we know
is that we cannot really be together
caught in the teeth of the machinery
of the wrong moments of our lives.

A clear umbilicus
goes out invisibly between,
thread we spin fluid and finer than hair
but strong enough to hang a bridge on.

That bridge will be there
a blacklight rainbow arching out of your skull
whenever you need
whenever you can open your eyes and want
to walk upon it.

Nobody can live on a bridge
or plant potatoes
but it is fine for comings and goings,
meetings, partings and long views
and a real connection to someplace else
where you may
in the crazy weathers of struggle
now and again want to be.

## Doing it differently

### 1.

Trying to enter each other,
trying to interpenetrate and let go.
Trying not to lie down in the same old rutted bed
part rack, part cocoon.
We are bagged in habit
like clothes back from the cleaners.
The map of your veins has been studied,
your thighs have been read and reported,
a leaden mistrust of the rhetoric of tenderness
thickens your tongue.
At the worst you see old movies in my eyes.
How can I persuade you that every day we choose
to give birth, to murder or feed our friends, to die a little.

### 2.

You are an opening in me.
Smoke thick as pitch blows in,
a wind bearing ribbons of sweet rain,
and the sun as field of dandelions, as rusty razor blade.
Scent colors the air with tear gas, with lemon lilies.

Most of the time you are not here.
Most of the time we wear different faces.
Mostly I do not touch you.
Mostly I am talking to someone else.

I crawl into you, a bee furry with greed
into the deep trumpeting throat of a crimson lily
speckled like a newly hatched robin.
I roll, heavy with nectar.
Later, I will turn this afternoon into honey
and live on it, frugally.
It will sweeten my tea.

3.
In the pit of the night our bodies merge,
dark clouds passing through each other in lightning,
the joining of rivers far underground in the stone.
I feel thick but hollow, a polyp floating on currents.
My nerves have opened wide mouths
to drink you in and sing O O on the dark
till I cannot fix boundaries where you start and I stop.
Then you are most vulnerable.
In me that nakedness does not close by day.
My quick, wound, door, my opening,
my lidless eye.

Don't you think it takes trust,
your strength, your temper always
in the room with us like a doberman leashed.
I fear being manipulated
by that touch point between us.

Touch is the primal sense—
for in the womb we swam lapped and tingling.

Fainting, practicing death, we lose
sight first, then hearing, the mouth and nose deaden
but still till the end we can touch.

Trust flourishes like a potato plant, mostly underground:
wan flowers, dusty leaves chewed by beetles,
but under the mulch as we dig
at every node of the matted tangle
the tubers, egg-shaped and golden with translucent skin,
tumble from the dirt to feed us
homely and nourishing.

4.

The Digger Indians were too primitive,
pushed onto the sparse alkaline plateau,
to make pottery that could stand on the fire.
They used to make soup by heating an oval stone
and dropping it in the pot cracking hot.
When traders came and sold them iron kettles
the women found cooking easier
but said the soup never tasted so good again.

Soup stone
blunt, heavy in my hands,
you soak, you hold, you radiate warmth,
you can serve as a weapon,
you can be used again and again
and you give a flavor to things I could miss.

5.

Beds that are mirrors,
beds that are rotisseries where I am the barbecue,
beds that are athletic fields for the Olympic trials,
beds that are dartboards, beds that are dentist's chairs,
beds that are consolation prizes floating on chicken soup,
beds where lobotomies are haphazardly performed,
beds of wet spaghetti, beds
that ride glittering through lies like a ferris wheel,
all the beds where a woman and a man
try to steal each other's bones
and call it love.

You do not want to say that word
yet that small commitment floating on a sea of spilled blood
has meaning if we inflict it.
Otherwise we fail into dry accommodation.
If we do not build a new loving out of our rubble
We will fall into a bamboo-staked trap on a lush trail.
You will secrete love out of old semen and gum and dreams.
What we do not remake
plays nostaglic songs on the jukebox of our guts,
and leads us into the old comfortable temptation.

6.

You lay in bed depressed, passive as butter.
I brought you a rose I had grown. You said
the rose was me, dark red and perfumed and three-quarters open,
soft as sometimes with embarrassment you praise my skin.

You talked of fucking the rose. Then you grew awkward;
we would never be free of roles, dominance and submission,
we slam through the maze of that pinball machine forever.

I say the rose is a place where we make love.
I am a body beautiful only when fitted with yours.
Otherwise, it walks, it lifts packages, it spades.
It is functional or sick, tired or sturdy. It serves.
Together we are the rose, full, red as the inside
of the womb and head of the penis,
blossoming as we encircle, we make that symmetrical fragrant emblem,
then separate into discreet workday selves.
The morning mail is true. Tomorrow's picketline is true.
And the rose, the rose of our loving
crimson, and sonorous as a cello
bowing on the curve of our spines, is true.

7.
We will be equal, we say, new man and new woman.
But what man am I equal to before the law of court or custom?
The state owns my womb and hangs a man's name on me
like the tags hung on dogs, my name is, property of. . . .
The language betrays us and rots in the mouth
with its aftertaste of monastic sewers on the palate.
Even the pronouns tear my tongue with their metal plates.

You could strangle me: my hands
can't even encircle your neck.
Because I open my mouth wide and stand up roaring
I am the outlawed enemy of men.
A party means what a bullfight does to the bull.
The street is a gauntlet.

56

I open my mail with tongs.
All the images of strength in you, fathers and prophets and heroes,
pull against me, till what feels right to you
wrongs me, and there is no rest from struggle.

We are equal if we make ourselves so, every day, every night
constantly renewing what the street destroys.
We are equal only if you open too on your heavy hinges
and let your love come freely, freely, where it will never be safe,
where you can never possess.

8.
For part of each month regularly as my period
I crave you.
When we mesh badly, with scraping and squeaking,
remember that every son had a mother
whose beloved son he was,
and every woman had a mother
whose beloved son she wasn't.
What feels natural and easy, is soft murder
of each other and that mutant future
striving to break into bloom
bloody and red as the real rose.

Periodic, earthy, of a violent tenderness
it is the nature of this joining
to remain partial and episodic
yet feel total: a mountain that opens like a door
and then closes
like a mountain.

### When will we sit down together?

Yesterday I thought suddenly of the summer of '68.
Retamar and Saul Yelin reminisced over wine—
street fights and demonstrations and faces of dead comrades.
It struck me hard, cozy at the cafe table,
they have had their revolution,
their own revolution.

For movement people to visit Cuba—
mugshot by the CIA in Mexico City airport,
chugging on bumpy Air Cubana with the passengers singing
and daiquiris handed up the aisle
out through the official hole in the blockade,
is like Dante getting swooped up by Beatrice
and carried—to Buddhist heaven.
It's glorious but it's theirs.
We have to make our own.
And it hurts to go home.

You I wrestle over the mimeograph machine,
you whose faces I see nowhere but in dreams,
when will we sit at our table?

I ask only for everything! To live long enough
to camp over wine in a cafe in free Nueva York
telling stories about the '70's
while in the streets children are playing loudly
together with laughter like ours
years ago in 1967
when our struggle was green and a game.
Now we ripen around the stone of first defeat.
Our flowers are past but our harvest is still to be won.

## What to chant under my breath

I turned and walked back into myself
but someone had taken the furniture.
My steps tapped echoes on the bare floors.
Switches clicked under my hand.
The faucet spat nothing explosively.
The phone was dead.

Fear is the mindsucker.
Fear is the gray destroyer.
Fog of fear drifting films the eyes.
Teeth of mice at every pore.
Slimes the voice.
Slacks the legs.
Sucks dry the marrow
till the bones all whistle
fluting bones
keening bones
and the only message is fear.

Born of the sea and dirt
to struggle and return,
now I will remember to draw air deeply.
Anger will warm my flesh.
My hands are crows,
my spine leaps and crackles
and the mind's sky will clear.

Fear is the mindsucker.
Fear is the gray destroyer.
Fear is the cold eater,
the still center of crouch.
Gray eye blinded,
gray hand shaking.
Fear is the suppliant's color.
Fear is the passive,
the shape of kneeling,
the shudder of plead.
Throat slams.
Genitals locked.
The nerves shut tight,
keep out! keep out!
Fear locks each into solitary
sucking a cold thumb.

All predators prefer a dinner that does not fight.
I won't be swallowed limp and mute
into the python belly of the state.
Fighting together can feel like work well done
singing on the body's trumpet.
Being eaten slowly is always a drag.

I will draw air deeply till my lungs unfold.
My spine stands rippling like grass.
Hands unclench to touch you
and the mind's good sky will clear.

Like the lion and the newt,
like the zebra and the pilot whale
we are made of sea and sun
and will return.
Now I go on and on a while.
Now I go on.

# The spring offensive of the snail

Living someplace else is wrong
in Jerusalem the golden
floating over New England smog,
above paper company forests,
deserted brick textile mills
square brooders on the rotten rivers,
developer-chewed mountains.

Living out of time is wrong.
The future drained us thin as paper.
We were tools scraping.
After the revolution
we would be good, love one another
and bake fruitcakes.
In the meantime eat your ulcer.

Living upside down is wrong,
roots in the air
mouths filled with sand.
Only what might be sang.
I cannot live crackling
with electric rage always.
The journey is too long
to run, cursing those
who can't keep up.

Give me your hand.
Talk quietly to everyone you meet.
It is going on.
We are moving again
with our houses on our backs.
This time we have to remember
to sing and make soup.
Pack the *Kapital* and the vitamin E,
the basil plant for the sill,
Apache tears you
picked up in the desert.

But remember to bury
all old quarrels
behind the garage for compost.
Forgive who insulted you.
Forgive yourself for being wrong.
You will do it again
for nothing living
resembles a straight line,
certainly not this journey
to and fro, zigzagging
you there and me here
making our own road onward
as the snail does.

Yes, for some time we might contemplate
not the tiger, not the eagle or grizzly
but the snail who always remembers
that wherever you find yourself eating
is home, the center
where you must make your love,
and wherever you wake up
is here, the right place to be
where we start again.

## Councils

(for two voices, female and male)

♀ :  We must sit down
      and reason together.
      We must sit down.
      Men standing want to hold forth.
      They rain down upon faces lifted.

♂ :  We must sit down on the floor
      on the earth
      on stones and mats and blankets.
      There must be no front to the speaking
      no platform, no rostrum,
      no stage or table.
      We will not crane
      to see who is speaking.

♀ :  Perhaps we should sit in the dark.
      In the dark we could utter our feelings.
      In the dark we could propose
      and describe and suggest.
      In the dark we could not see who speaks
      and only the words
      would say what they say.

♂ :  No one would speak more than twice,
      no one would speak less than once.

♀ : Thus saying what we feel and what we want,
what we fear for ourselves and each other
into the dark, perhaps we could begin
to begin to listen.

♂ : Perhaps we should talk in groups
the size of new families,
never more than twenty.

♀ : Perhaps we should start by speaking softly.
The women must learn to dare to speak.

♂ : The men must bother to listen.

♀ : The women must learn to say, I think this is so.

♂ : The men must learn to stop dancing solos on the ceiling.
After each speaks, she or he
will repeat a ritual phrase:

♀ & ♂ : It is not I who speaks but the wind.
Wind blows through me.
Long after me, is the wind.

# III. LAYING DOWN THE TOWER

# *LAYING DOWN THE TOWER*

These eleven poems are the cards of a Tarot reading.

As in any reading, the significator is chosen—the card I identify with —and the other cards choose themselves. As in any reading, the context of the total set works on the way individual cards are interpreted.

As with other magical elements in subculture, the ways we learn to read the cards from friends or the books we may read about the Tarot contain heavy bourgeois elements. Now, every reading of the cards implies judgments—a valuing of some things and a putting down of others. Every reading implies a clumping of ideas about self and others, about good and bad, about female and male, about what winning and losing mean.

This reading is political: the values are different than in more conventional ways of reading the deck. But they're not any more present than in the ways that say the Nine of Cups is a fortunate card because it means you get a whole lot of "goods," to have and hold.

We must break through the old roles to encounter our own meanings in the symbols we experience in dreams, in songs, in vision, in meditation. Some of these symbols are much older than capitalism, and some contain knowledge we must recover; but we receive all through a filter that has aligned the stuff by values not our own.

What we use we must remake. Then only we are not playing with dead dreams but seeing ourselves more clearly, and more clearly becoming. The defeated in history lose their names, their goddesses, their language, their culture. The myths we imagine we are living (old westerns, true romances) shape our choices.

Some of the most significant myths are those of history. Here I am reconciling myself to my own history and trying to bring my sense of that history to you. I find current media and official formulas about the recent past lethal. I experience them as an assault, a robbery. At the same time in my third movement, I go through a sense of ghostly recurrence, of centrifugal forces and schisms that unnecessarily rack and divide. Each succeeding movement has been for me a qualitative change in depth of personal involvement, in perception of the world, in what I want; the totality of the struggle in the women's movement has shaken me and altered me past the level of conscious mind. But trying to write our own history is of mutual concern, for if we cannot learn from that recent past and each other, we become our worst rhetoric. Whatever is not an energy source, is an energy sink.

### *The Significator, The Querent:*
### *THE QUEEN OF PENTACLES*

This is my deck I unwrap, and this is the card for me.
I will in any house find quickly like my sister the cat
the most comfortable chair, snug out of drafts.
Empathy flows through my fingers:
I need to touch.
I am at home in that landscape of unkempt garden,
mulch and manure, thorny blackberry and sunflower and grape coiling,
tomato plants mad with fecundity bending their stakes,
asparagus waving fronds in the wind.

Even in a New York apartment with dirt
bought in bags like chocolate candy, I raised herbs.
I prefer species roses rough as weeds
with a strong scent, simple flowers and hips good for jam.
I like wine's fine weather on my palate.
I can sink into my body like a mole
and be lost in the tunnels of the nerves, suckling.
I want to push roots deep in my hillside and sag with ripeness,
an apple tree sprawling with fruit.

The music sacred to me speaks through drums
directly on my pulses, into the chambers of my brain.
Yet this knowing is hard and bloody, that should dance through us.
Too many have been murdered from the sky,
the soil has been tainted and blows away and the water stinks.

I want to grow into the benign mother with open hands
healing and fertile but must spay myself to serve,
sear off one breast like an Amazon to fight
for even the apple that shines in the hand
is secretly waxed and full of poison.
The orange is dyed with the blood of the picker.
The peach plucked green tastes of paper dollars,
run off by the emperor to finance his wars.

How often my own words set my teeth on edge
sour and hard, tearing the roof of my mouth.
What I do well and what I must do make war in my chest.
Through other women sometimes I can touch
pruned selves, smothered wishes, small wet cries that vanished
and think how all together we make up one good strong woman.
Still to get strength
for the things we have to do that frighten me
I go and dig my hands into the ground.

### *The Matter:* **THE TOWER STRUCK BY LIGHTNING REVERSED;** *Also the Matter is* **THE OVERTURNING OF THE TOWER**

All my life I have been a prisoner under the Tower.
Some say that gray lid is the sky. Our streets are hammers.
Gray is the water we drink, gray the face I cannot love in the mirror,
gray is the money we lack, the itch and scratch of skins rubbing.
Gray is the color of work without purpose or end,
and the cancer of hopelessness creeping through the gut.

In my bones are calcium rings of the body's hunger
from gray bread that turns to ash in the belly.
In my brain schooled lies rot into self-hatred: and who
can I hate in the cattle car subway
like the neighbor whose elbow cracks my ribs?

The Tower of Baffle speaks bureaucratic and psychologese,
multiple choice, one in vain, one insane, one trite as rain.
Journalist in which each government repression is a reform.
Military bumblewords, pre-emptive stroke, mind and body count and
strategic omelet.
Above in the sun live those who own, making our weather with their
refuse.
Their neon signs instruct us through the permanent smog.
Rockefellers, Mellons and Duponts, you Fords and Houghtons,
who are you to own my eyes? Who gave me to be your serf?
I have never seen your faces but your walls surround me.
With the loot of the world you built these stinking cities as monuments.
The Tower is ugly as General Motors, as public housing,
as the twin piles of the World Trade Center spewing asbestos,
tallest, biggest and menacing as fins on an automobile,
horns on a Minotaur programmed to kill.

The weight of the Tower is in me. Can I ever straighten?
You trained me in passivity to lay for you like a doped hen.
You bounce your gabble off the sky to pierce our brains.
Your loudspeakers from every television and classroom
and your transistors grafted onto my nerves at birth
shout you are impregnable and righteous forever.
But any structure can be overthrown.

London Bridge with the woman built into the base
as sacrifice is coming down.
The Tower will fall if we pull together.
Then the Tower reversed, symbol of tyranny and oppression,
shall not be set upright.
We are not turning things over merely
but we will lay the Tower on its side.
We will make it a communal longhouse.

***That Which Crosses, That Which Opposes:***
***the Force Against the Overthrowing***
***of the Tower : THE NINE OF CUPS***

Not fat, not gross, just well fed and hefty he sits before what's his,
the owner, the ultimate consumer, the overlord.
No human kidneys can pump nine cups of wine through
but that's missing the point of having: possession is power
whether he owns apartment houses or herds of prime beef
or women's soft hands or the phone lines or the right to kill
or pieces of paper that channel men's working hours.

81

He is not malcontent. He has that huge high-colored
healthy face you see on executives just massaged.
He eats lobster, he drinks aged scotch, he buys pretty women.
He buys men who write books about how he is a servant of circumstance.
He buys armies to shoot peasants squatting on his oil.

He is your landlord: he shuts off the heat and the light and the water,
he shuts off air, he shuts off growth, he shuts off your sex.
He buys men who know geology for him, he buys men who count stars,
he buys women who paint their best dreams all over his ceiling.
He buys giants who grow for him and dwarfs who shrink
and he eats them all, he eats, he eats well,
he eats and twenty Bolivians starve, a division of labor.

You are in his cup, you float like an icecube, you sink like an onion.
Guilt is the training of his servants that we may serve harder.
His priests sell us penance for his guilt,
his psychiatrists whip our parents through our cold bowels,
his explainers drone of human nature and the human condition.

He is squatting on our heads laughing. He belches with health.
He feels so very good he rewards us with TV sets
which depict each one of us his servants sitting
just as fat and proud and ready to stomp
in front of the pile of tin cans we call our castle.

On the six o'clock news the Enemy attacks.
Then our landlord spares no expense to defend us,
for the hungry out there want to steal our TV sets.
He raises our taxes one hundred per cent
and sells us weapons and sends us out to fight.
We fight and we die, for god, country and the dollar
and then we come back home
and he raises the rent.

### *The Influence Passing, the Foundation or Base:*
### *THE KNIGHT OF SWORDS*

I was a weapon. I brandished myself, I was used in the air.
We rushed in waves at the Tower and were hurtled back.
Because we were right, should we not win?

85

When you know that in the external and internal colonies
people are dying of hunger, of napalm, of gas, of rats, of racism,
dying and dying each death is a drop of blood falling
all night on your forehead, each death is a nail tapped in.
It is participation in murder
to sit one moment longer at the key punch,
it is guilt by association to raise your hand in class,
it is being an accomplice to take a job in the lab.
Buying a car, you pay for a fragmentation bomb.

If you are not fighting, are you not supporting?
If you saw the children starving in Brazil, would you wait
the five minutes that is five more bodies bloating?
If you saw the children burning in the bombed villages of Laos
would you have another coffee and eat the jelly doughnut?
If you saw the inside of that prison, would you switch channels?

So run at the barricade and throw back the canister of gas.
So take the club in your face and keep on slugging.
We must win, we must win for everybody so we cannot,
we can never pause, we have no time to look, we cannot breathe.

Run, keep running, don't look sideways.
The blood is raining down all of the time, how can we rest?
How can we pause to think, how can we argue with you,
how can we pause to reason and win you over?
Conscience is the sword we wield,
conscience is the sword that runs us through.

***That Which is Now Behind, Previous Condition:***
  ***THE EIGHT OF SWORDS***

Bound, blinded, stymied, with bared blades for walls
and alone, my eyes and mouth filled up with dark.
We had grown used to Movement, that sense of thaw,
things breaking loose and openings and doors pushed by the wind,
spring after the end of the Age of Ice.
Used to feeling connected, used to sisters and brothers,
used to an us that felt bigger and warmer than them.

Without intelligence but stubborn and clumsy with theory
we grew like weeds in sand.
We lusted after brave loud crashing rhetoric
and threw small gains away because they made no show.
We clashed on each other, we chopped, we never hit harder
than when we were axing a comrade two feet to the right.
Factions charred our energies. Repression ground us.

Some they bought off, some they shot down,
some they locked in their prisons or their asylums,
some they wasted with their heroin pumped in the streets,
some they have broken in hospitals, some they have gagged,
some they tormented till we rushed into death screaming rage,
some they tricked into despair so we stood impaled:
no longer could we imagine winning.

Despair is the worst betrayal, the coldest seduction:
to believe at last that the enemy will prevail.
Hush, the heart's drum, my life, my breath.
There is finally a bone in the heart that does not break
when we remember we are still part of each other,
the muscle of hope that goes on in the dark
pumping the blood that feeds us.

### *The Influence Coming into Play:*
### *THE SEVEN OF PENTACLES*

Under a sky the color of pea soup
she is looking at her work growing away there
actively, thickly like grapevines or pole beans
as things grow in the real world, slowly enough.

89

If you tend them properly, if you mulch, if you water,
if you provide birds that eat insects a home and winter food,
if the sun shines and you pick off caterpillars,
if the praying mantis comes and the ladybugs and the bees,
then the plants flourish, but at their own internal clock.

Connections are made slowly, sometimes they grow underground.
You cannot tell always by looking what is happening.
More than half a tree is spread out in the soil under your feet.
Penetrate quietly as the earthworm that blows no trumpet.
Fight persistently as the creeper that brings down the tree.
Spread like the squash plant that overruns the garden.
Gnaw in the dark and use the sun to make sugar.

Weave real connections, create real nodes, build real houses.
Live a life you can endure: make love that is loving.
Keep tangling and interweaving and taking more in,
a thicket and bramble wilderness to the outside but to us
interconnected with rabbit runs and burrows and lairs.

Live as if you liked yourself, and it may happen:
reach out, keep reaching out, keep bringing in.
This is how we are going to live for a long time: not always,
for every gardener knows that after the digging, after the planting,
after the long season of tending and growth, the harvest comes.

\

### *The Aim, the Best that Can Be Hoped for:*
### *THE MAGICIAN*

Fusion is miracle and there is no other way, it is necessary.
Every new age is unbelievable beforehand and after, inevitable.
History is a game played backwards only.

I fling my eyes into the maw of the sun.
With all our strength, we thrust into fierce light.
We are yearning like frogs bulging our throats in the spring marsh
and croaking harsh and ridiculous spasms of hope.
I tell you, roses want to bloom out of the wood,
the goodness in people wants to break free
of the blind ego.
Birth is a miracle in every germinating seed.

We had thought we were waiting our Messiah, our Lenin,
our golden Organizer who would fuse us into one body
but now we see when we grow heads they lop them off.
We must be every one the connection between energy and mass,
every one the lightning that strikes to topple the tower,
each must conduct light, heat and crackling strength
into each other: we must open a thousand fiery eyes and mouths
of flame that make us visible and pass to others.

The lion arches in my back, the goat kicks in my legs.
You skim, a glinting dragonfly, into my head and we couple in air.
Each time we say *sisters*,
each time you say *brothers*, we are making magic
for we were born each to scream alone, a worm in armor,
trained to grab at all and cherish nothing.

Every soul must become a magician; the magician is in touch.
The magician connects. The magician helps each thing
to open into what it truly wants to utter.
The saying is not the magic: we have drunk words and eaten
manifestoes and grown bloated on resolutions
and farted winds of sour words that left us weak.
It is in the acting with the strength we cannot
really have till we have won.

Give birth to me, sisters, in struggle we transform
ourselves, but how often, how often
we need help to cut loose, to cry out, to breathe!
In his head, floating on drugs, everybody is born again good
but how hard to make that miracle pass in the streets.
This morning we must make each other strong.
Change is qualitative: we are
each other's miracle.

***Querent's Attitude as it Bears upon the Matter:***
   ***THE THREE OF CUPS***


A poem is a dancing: it goes out of a mouth to your ears
and for some moments aligns us,
so we wheel and turn together.
The blackbirds dance over the marsh as they drive off the hawk.
The marsh hawks hunt in spirals paired, crying.
The bees dance where the pollen is to be gathered, and dance their fierce
                                                            mating.

When I dance I forget myself, I am danced.
Music fills me to overflowing and the power moves
up from my feet to my fingers, making leaves as sap does.

My dance is of you: we are dancing together though scattered,
atomistic as Brownian motes, the same music holds us.
Even after Altamont, even after we have discovered
we are still death's darling children, born of the print-out,
the laser, the war-game, the fragmentation weapons of education,
still we must bear joy back into the world.
We must rise up in joy and endurance,
we must shake off the oil of passivity and no more be spectators
even before the masque of our own dark and bright dreams.

We grew up in Disneyland with ads for friends
and believed we could be made new by taking a pill.
We wanted instant revolution, where all we had to add
was a little smoke.
There is no tribe who dance and then sit down
and wait for the crops to harvest themselves
and supper to roll over before the pot.
We shall survive only if we win; they will kill us
if they can, and killing is what they do best.
We have learned to do nothing well.
We are still strangers to our bodies,
tools fit awkwardly in our hands, our weapons explode,
we speak to each other haltingly in words they gave us.

Taste what is in your mouth,
if it is water, still taste it.
Wash out the cups of your fingers,
clean your eyes with new tears for your sister.
We are not worse revolutionaries if we remember
that the universe itself pulses like a heart;
that the blood dances within us; that joy is a power
treading with hoofs and talons on our flimsy bodies;
that water flows and fire leaps and the land gives strength
if you build on it with respect, if you dance on it with vigor,
if you put seeds in with care and give back what is left over;
that a ritual of unity makes some of what it pretends;
that every thing is a part of something else.

### *The House, The Environment:*
### *THE EMPEROR*

In the house of power grown old but unyielding
the emperor sits severe in mail, watching all that creep;
even over the grasshoppers and the minnows and the leaves
that catch sun into food, he wields barrenness.
He holds a globe like something he might bite into
and an ankh, for he will carry his dominion into the living cells
and the ancient cabala of the genes he plans to revise
till everything born is programmed to obey.

The Man from Mars with sterile mountains at his back—
perhaps strip-mined, perhaps the site of weapons testing—
if we opened that armor like a can, would we find a robot?
quaking old flesh? the ghost of an inflated bond issue?

Evil old men banal as door knobs
who rule the world like a comic strip,
you are the Father Who Eats His Young,
the final purity of the Male Principle of corner and kill.
Power abhors a vacuum, you say and sit down at the Wurlitzer
to play the color organ of poison gases.
All roads lead to the top of the pyramid on the dollar bill
where hearts are torn out and skulls split to feed
the ultimate ejaculating machine, the ruling class climax by missile.
The gnats of intelligence who have bugged every pay toilet
in the country, sing in your beard of court cases and jails to come.
It is reason enough to bomb a village if it cannot be bought.
Heavy as dinosaurs, plated and armored,
you crush the land under your feet and flatten it,
lakes of smoking asphalt spread where your feet have trod.

You exiled the Female into blacks and women and colonies.
You became the armed brain and the barbed penis and the club.
You invented agribusiness, leaching the soil to dust,
and pissed mercury in the rivers and shat slag on the plains,
withered your emotions to ulcers,
strait-jacketed the mysteries and sent them to shock therapy.
Your empress is a new-model car with breasts.

100

There is in the dance of all things together no profit
for each feeds the next and all pass through each other,
the serpent whose tail is in her mouth,
our mother earth turning.
Now the wheel of the seasons sticks and the circle is broken
and life spills out in an oil slick to rot the seas.
You are the God of the Puritans playing war games on computers:
you can give birth to nothing
except death.

### *What Is Most Hoped and/or Most Feared in the Matter: THE JUDGMENT*

I call on the dead, I call on the defeated, on the starved,
the sold, the tortured, the executed, the robbed:
Indian women bayoneted before their children at Sand Creek,
miners who choked on the black lung,
strikers shot down at Pullman and Republic Steel,
women bled to death of abortions men made illegal,
sold, penned in asylums, lobotomized, raped and torn open,
every black killed by police, national guard, mobs and armies.
Live in us: give us your strength, give us your counsel,
give us your rage and your will to come at last into the light.

I fear the trial, I fear the struggle, it parches and withers me.
I fear the violence into whose teeth we march.
I long for the outcome with every cheated cell.
We shall all waken finally to being human.

I was trained to be numb, I was born to be numbered and pegged,
I was bred and conditioned to passivity, like a milk cow.
Waking is the sharpest pain I have ever known.
Every barrier that goes down takes part of my flesh
leaving me bloody. How can I live wide open?

Why must I think of you and you before I take a bite?
Why must I look to my sister before I scratch my itch?
Before, I shuffled and giggled and kept my eyes down,
tucking my shoulders in so I would not rub the walls
of the rut, the place, the role.
Now anger blisters me.
My pride rumbles, sputtering lava.
Every day is dangerous and glad.

*"Why do you choose to be noisy, to fight, to make trouble?"*
you ask me, not understanding I have been born raw and new.
I can be killed with ease, I can be cut right down,
but I cannot crawl back in the cavern
where I lay with my neck bowed.
I have grown. I am not by myself.
I am too many.

### *The Total Influence or Outcome*
### *of the Matter: THE SUN*

Androgynous child whose hair curls into flowers,
naked you ride a horse without saddle or bridle
easy between your thighs from the walled garden outward.
Coarse sunflowers of desire whose seeds birds crack open
nod upon your journey, child of the morning whose sun
can only be born from us who strain bleeding to give birth.
Grow into your horse, let there be
no more riders or ridden.

Child, where are you heading with arms spread wide
as a shore, have I been there, have I seen that land shining
like sun spangles on clean water rippling?
I do not know your dances, I cannot translate your tongue
to words I use, your pleasures are strange to me
as the rites of bees: yet you are the yellow flower
of a melon vine growing out of my belly
though it climbs up where I cannot see in the strong light.

My eyes cannot decipher those shapes of children or burning clouds
who are not what we are: they go barefoot like savages,
they have computers as household pets; they are seven sexes
and only one sex; they do not own or lease or control.
They are of one body and of tribes. They are private as shamans
learning each her own magic at the teats of stones and trees.
They are all technicians and peasants.
They do not forget their birthright of self
or their mane of animal pride
dancing in and out through the gates of the body standing wide.

A bear lumbering, I waddle into the fields of their work games.
We are stunted slaves mumbling over the tales
of dragons our masters tell us, but we will be free.
Our children will be free of us uncomprehending
as we of those shufflers in caves who scraped for fire
and banded together at last to hunt the saber-toothed tiger,
the tusked mastodon, the giant cave bear,
predators that had penned them up cowering so long.

The sun is rising, feel it: the air smells fresh.
I cannot look in the sun's face, its brightness blinds me,
but from my own shadow becoming distinct
I know that now at last
it is beginning to grow light.

λ